CRAFTS
for kids

Beads

Greta Speechley

WAYLAND

This edition published in 2007 by Wayland

Wayland
338 Euston Road
London NW1 3BH

Wayland Australia
Hachette Children's Books
Level 17/207 Kent Street
Sydney, NSW 2000

For The Brown Reference Group plc.
Craftperson: Greta Speechley
Project Editor: Jane Scarsbrook
Designer: Joan Curtis
Photography: Martin Norris
Design Manager: Lynne Ross
Managing Editor: Bridget Giles
Editorial Director: Lindsey Lowe

British Library Cataloguing in Publication Data

Speechley, Greta, 1948–
  Beads. - (Crafts for kids)
  1. Beadwork - Juvenile literature
  I. Title
  745.5'82

ISBN-13: 9780750251587

ISBN: 978-0-7502-5158-7

Printed and bound in Thailand

Wayland is a division of Hachette Children's Books

Contents

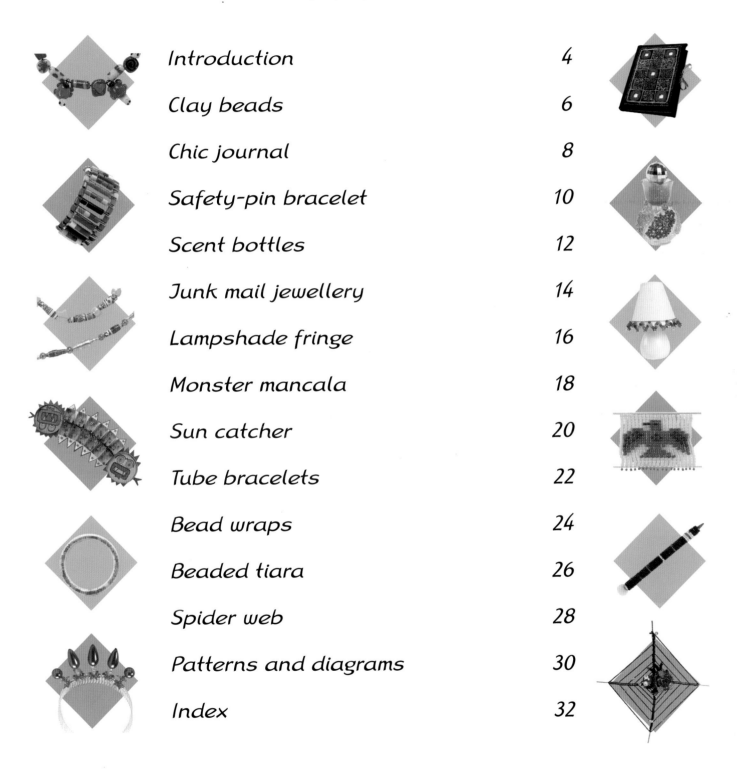

Introduction

This book is packed with brilliant bead crafts. You can make funky beads from junk mail and tiny turtle beads from clay. Use glass beads to make a scent bottle sparkle, and collect plastic beads in rainbow colours to make safety-pin bracelets. If you've got some beads left over, learn to play mancala with bead counters and make a beady-eyed spider, too!

YOU WILL NEED

Each project includes a list of all the things you need. Before you buy new materials, look at home to see what you could use instead. For example, save up small matchboxes so you have enough to make the mancala game. You can buy plastic tubing and wooden dowels from a hardware shop and small embroidered mirrors from a fabric store. You're bound to have beads at home, but visit a bead shop to find more in every size and colour.

Getting started

 Read the steps for the project first.

 Gather together all the items you need.

Cover your work surface with newspaper.

 Wear an apron, or change into old clothes.

A message for adults

All the projects in *Beads* have been designed for children to make, but occasionally they will need you to help. Some of the projects do require the use of sharp utensils, such as scissors or needles. Please read through the instructions for the project before your child starts work.

Patterns and diagrams

Follow these steps to make the patterns on page 30. Using a pencil, trace the pattern onto tracing paper. To cut the pattern out of paper, turn the tracing over, and lay it on to the paper. Rub firmly over the pattern with a pencil. The shape will appear on the paper. Cut out the shape. There are also diagrams on pages 30 and 31 to help you with the Sun catcher project on pages 20 and 21 and the Lampshade fringe on pages 16 and 17.

When you have finished

Wash paintbrushes and put everything away.

Put pens, pencils, paints and glue in an old box or ice cream container.

Keep scissors and other sharp items in a safe place.

Stick needles and pins into a pincushion or a piece of scrap cloth.

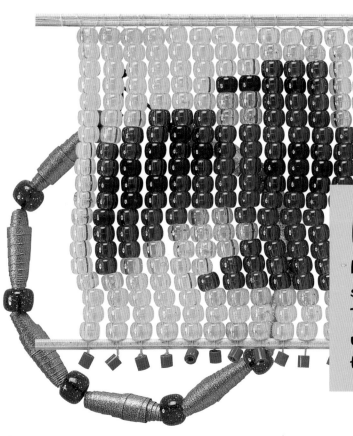

BE SAFE

Look out for the safety boxes. They will appear whenever you need to ask an adult for help.

Ask an adult to help you use sharp scissors.

Clay beads

Clay is great for making beads.
Try making animal beads, car and
aeroplane beads and alphabet
beads. You can string them on
to wristbands, shoelaces
or necklaces.

YOU WILL NEED

red, yellow, blue and black oven-hardening clay	clay varnish small paintbrush wire (we've used florist's wire)
toothpicks	
elastic cord	
scissors	clay cutter or plastic knife

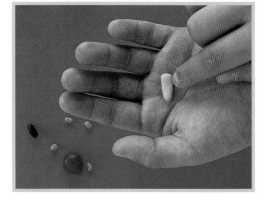

1 To make a turtle bead, roll out a ball of red clay for the body. Roll out four tiny blue balls for the feet and a yellow sausage for the head. Make a tail from black clay.

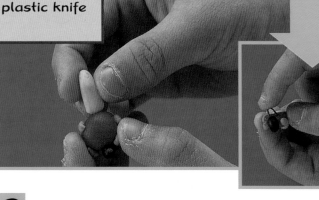

2 Gently press the pieces together to make the turtle. Stick on two black dots for eyes. Make a small loop of wire and push it into the turtle so that you will be able to thread it on to a necklace.

6

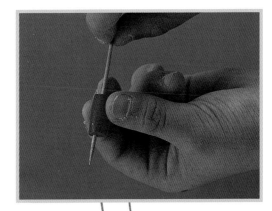

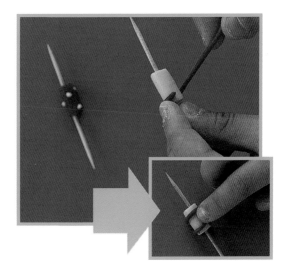

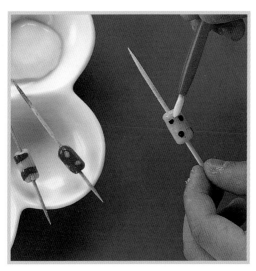

3 To make two tube-shaped beads, roll out a short, fat sausage of red clay and one of yellow clay. Use a toothpick to poke a hole through the centre of each bead.

4 Wind a thin sausage of red clay around the yellow bead to make stripes. Press dots of yellow clay on to the red bead. Roll the beads with your finger to flatten the surface. Make lots of beads and ask an adult to bake them, following the instructions on the clay package.

5 When the beads have been baked and cooled, paint them with clay varnish to make them shiny. Let them dry.

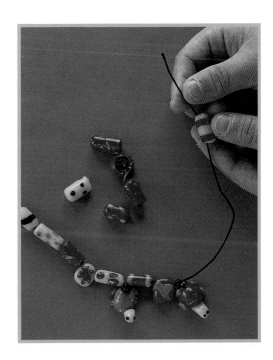

Ask an adult to bake the clay beads.

6 Thread your beads on to elastic cord to make a colourful necklace.

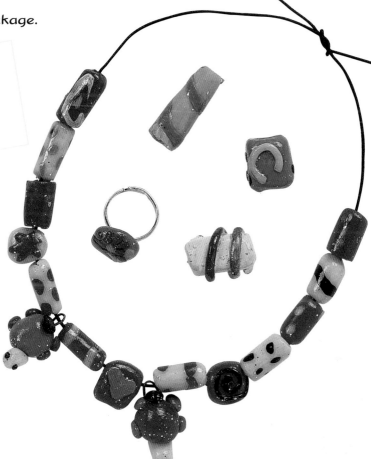

Chic journal

Use tiny mirrors and glass beads to turn any old notebook into a chic journal for all your thoughts and plans.

YOU WILL NEED

- small hardback book
- black felt for the cover
- chalk
- scissors
- red felt for the inside
- gold ribbon for ties
- gold thread
- small mirrors from a craft shop
- assorted small beads
- fabric glue
- red fabric
- glitter pen
- toothpick

1 Lay the open notebook on a piece of black felt. Cut around the edge leaving a 5 cm (2 in) margin. Draw a diagonal chalk line at each corner about 1.25 cm (½ in) out from the corner so that when you close the book, the jacket fits.

2 Cut off the corners of the felt, and cut a V-shape at the top and bottom of the book's spine. Glue the flaps into the front and back covers.

8

4 Draw a grid of 15 squares on to the front cover of the book using fabric glue. Press gold thread down along the glue trail.

3 Cut two pieces of red felt the same size as the book's cover. Glue a ribbon on to the inside of the front and back covers. Glue the red felt on top.

5 Glue small mirrors with decorative borders into the corner squares and the centre square.

6 Dab fabric glue into one of the free squares. Drop in beads and press them down gently. Use a toothpick to position the beads more carefully. Fill in all the free squares with beads. Draw a red outline around the grid using a fabric glitter pen.

Safety-pin bracelet

This cheerful bracelet is such fun to wear. Try making a sparkly safety-pin bracelet with small glass beads instead of coloured plastic beads. In place of the extra bead between each pin, thread on an upside-down pin.

YOU WILL NEED

20 safety pins the same size
plastic beads
elastic cord
scissors

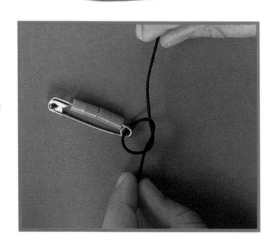

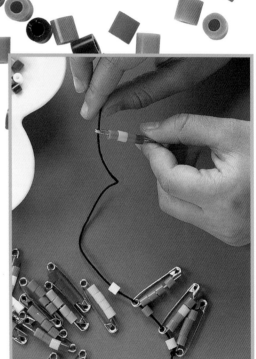

1 Thread four beads on to the point of a safety pin, and close the pin. Make 20 beaded pins like this. We have made 10 threaded with different-coloured beads and 10 with beads of the same colour. Tie elastic cord to the bottom circle of one beaded pin.

2 Thread all 20 pins onto the elastic by their bottom circle. Between each pin thread on an extra bead. Make sure the beaded sides of the pins point the same way. We have threaded on a multi-coloured pin and then a one-colour pin all the way along.

10

3 When you have threaded all the pins on, tie a loose knot around the last extra bead to keep the pins in place.

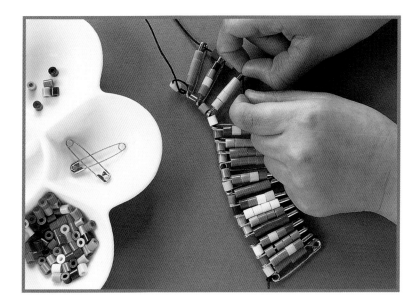

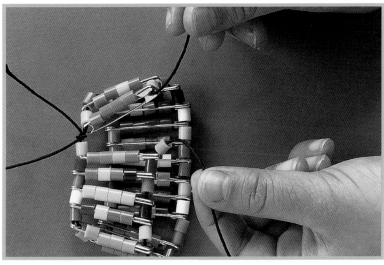

4 Thread a second piece of elastic through the top circles in the pins. Again, thread on an extra bead between each pin. Push the pins into line and check that they are all the right way around.

5 Tie the elastic ends at the top and bottom as securely as you can.

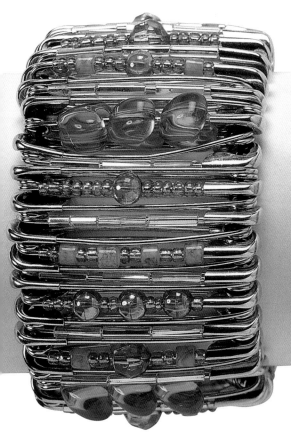

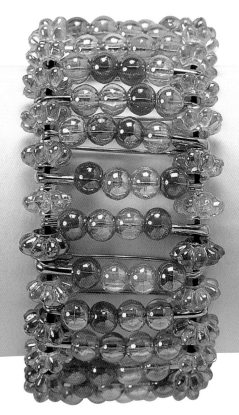

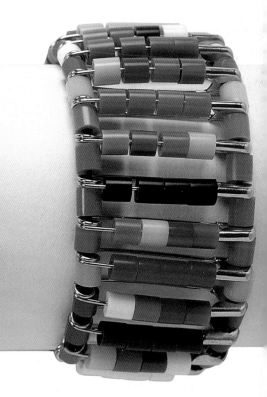

Scent bottles

Look out for a small bottle with a nice shape and an unusual lid. Use a mixture of glass paints and beading to make a pretty bottle for your favourite scent.

YOU WILL NEED

small bottle	strong clear
small beads in	glue
four different	gold glass
colours	paint
light blue	large gold
plastic	bead
beads	toothpick

1 Draw the outline of your pattern on to the bottle using gold glass paint. We have drawn a wiggly line around the bottle near the neck, one near the bottom and diagonal lines between the two to make four sections. Let the glass paint dry.

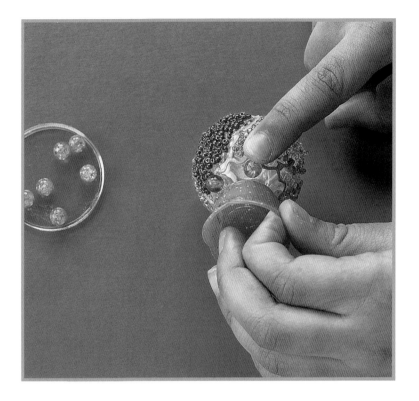

2 Dab glue over one section of the bottle and drop on small beads. Press down gently. You can use a toothpick to push the beads into position. Let each section dry before you move on to the next.

3 We have put pink beads in one section, then yellow in the next. Fill the other two sections with blue beads and then green beads. Glue on a ring of larger blue beads near the neck of the bottle.

4 To finish off, you could glue a large gold bead to the lid of the bottle. This round bottle looks lovely, but a bottle with flat sides is easier to work on. Let each side dry before you bead the next.

Junk mail jewellery

You can use old comics, coloured scrap paper or junk mail to make these multi-coloured paper beads.

1 Use a ruler to make marks every 2.5 cm (1 in) along the edge of a piece of scrap coloured paper. Between these marks make smaller marks every 1.25 cm (½ in). Do the same along the opposite edge.

YOU WILL NEED

scrap comic paper or junk mail	round coloured plastic beads
felt-tip pen	wooden skewer or knitting needle
ruler	
scissors	
paper glue	PVA glue and paintbrush
elastic cord	

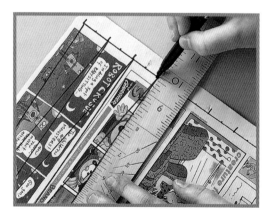

2 Rule diagonal lines from the big marks along one edge to the small marks along the other to make a pattern like the one above.

14

3 Cut out the long, thin triangles of paper, following the lines you have drawn.

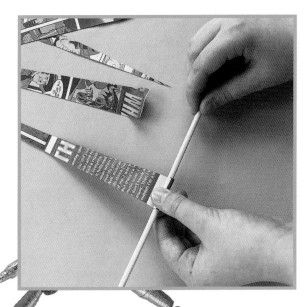

4 Starting at the wide end of the triangle, wind it up around a wooden skewer. Roll it evenly to make a neat bead.

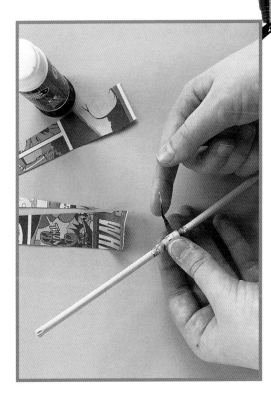

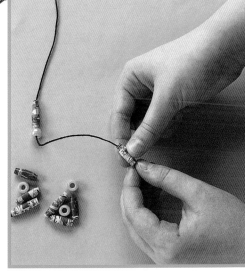

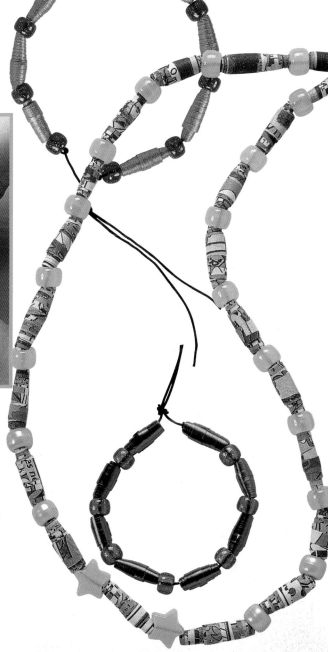

5 Glue down the thin tip at the end of the triangle. Let the glue dry and then slip off the bead. Make lots more beads.

6 You can varnish the beads by painting them with PVA glue. Let them dry. Thread the paper beads onto a long piece of elastic with a coloured plastic bead in between each one. Ask a friend to tie it around your neck and to trim off the extra elastic.

Lampshade fringe

This circle of threaded beads goes over a lampshade to make a fringe. Choose coloured see-through beads, and they will glow in the lamplight.

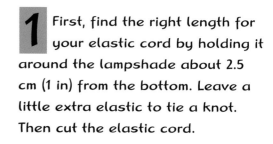

1 First, find the right length for your elastic cord by holding it around the lampshade about 2.5 cm (1 in) from the bottom. Leave a little extra elastic to tie a knot. Then cut the elastic cord.

YOU WILL NEED

nylon thread
elastic cord
round,
  see-through
  plastic beads
small lamp
  with shade
star-shaped
  see-through
  beads

small glass
beads (they
shouldn't be
so small that
they slip
through the
hole in the
star beads)

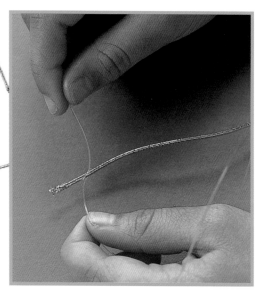

2 Take the cord off the lampshade. Tie the end of the nylon thread to one end of the elastic cord.

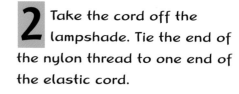

16

3 Thread on beads, following the diagram on page 30. First thread on four round beads. To make a V-shape, thread on a star bead and then a small bead. Push the nylon back through the star bead.

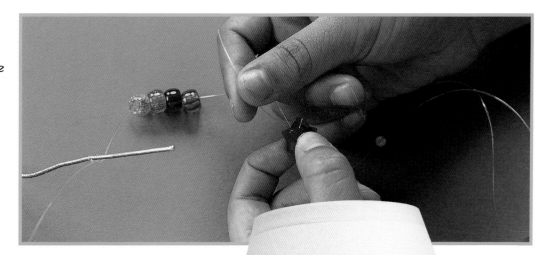

4 Thread on four more round beads. Loop the nylon over the cord, and thread it back through the fourth bead.

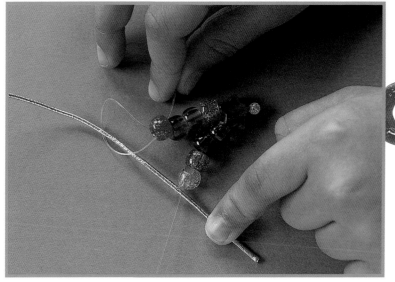

5 Repeat the bead pattern until you have filled the cord. Tie the beaded fringe around the lampshade so that it doesn't slip off.

Monster mancala

The object of this African game is to collect the most beads in your mancala. The mancala is the round pot at each end of the game board.

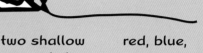

YOU WILL NEED

two shallow round cheese boxes
large piece of stiff cardboard
12 small matchboxes
poster paints
paintbrush
round plastic beads

red, blue, green, and pink coloured paper
compass
pencil
pinking shears
scissors
felt-tip pens
purple felt
tinsel

1 Arrange 12 small matchbox bases on a piece of stiff cardboard to make the monster's body. Place a round cheese box at either end for the monster's heads. Draw around the shape, adding spikes for hair. Then cut out the shape with scissors.

2 Take off the boxes, and paint the base yellow in the middle. Paint the two heads red. Paint the insides of the matchboxes orange and the insides of the round cheese boxes blue.

3 Glue the boxes in place. Trace the star patterns on page 30. Use the tracing to cut out 12 small stars from red paper. Glue them on to the hair spikes. Cut out 12 big stars from blue paper and glue them into the matchboxes.

4 Use a compass to measure the radius of the cheese boxes. Draw two circles with this radius on to coloured paper. Cut them out with pinking shears and draw on monster faces.

5 Glue a purple felt tongue to the bottom of the board at each end of the monster. Stick the monster faces into the round boxes. They should point in opposite directions, so one faces each player. Push tinsel between the matchboxes to make a monster spine.

HOW TO PLAY

The round pot on your right is your mancala. You also own the six boxes closest to you. Your friend sits on the other side of the board and owns the other mancala and boxes.

1 Place four beads in each box.

2 Start by scooping up all the beads from one of your boxes. Drop a bead into the box on the right, then a bead into the box after that — carry on around the board until you have run out of beads. You can drop a bead into your mancala, but you must skip your opponent's mancala.

3 If the last bead you drop goes into your mancala, take another turn. If the last bead goes into an empty box of yours, capture all the beads in the box opposite. Put them all in your mancala.

4 Take turns to play. The game ends when one player's boxes are all empty. The winner is the player with the most beads in his or her mancala.

19

Sun catcher

Collect see-through plastic beads to make this magnificent beaded eagle. Hang the eagle in your window so it catches the light and glows.

YOU WILL NEED

see-through nylon thread	see-through plastic beads:
ruler	209 yellow
scissors	122 blue
2 wooden skewers	23 red
	4 green
19 blue plastic starter beads	2 purple
	1 orange
glue	

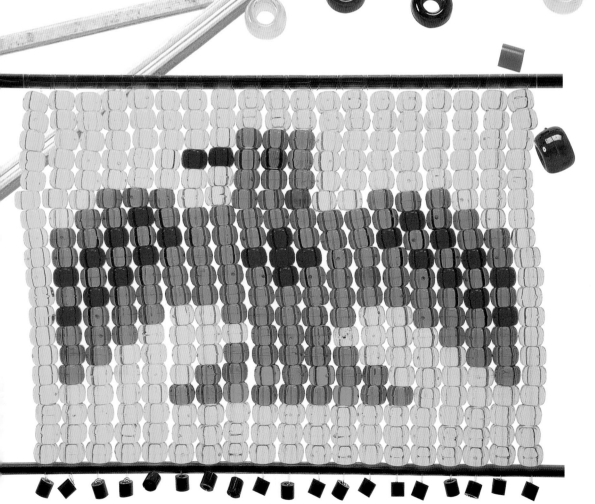

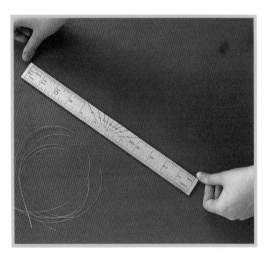

1 Measure 19 lengths of nylon thread, each 45.5 cm (18 in) long. Fold one in half and loop it over the wooden skewer as shown in the picture on the left.

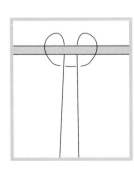

2 Follow the diagram on page 31 to make the eagle. For example, the diagram shows that you need to thread 19 yellow beads on to the first strand of nylon. Tie the thread to the bottom skewer to keep the beads in place. Knot it a few times. Tie on the second nylon strand.

3 Thread seven yellow beads on to the second nylon strand, then two blue, then one red, then one blue, then one red, then three blue, then four yellow. When you have threaded beads on to all 19 strands, you can see the picture of the eagle. Glue plastic starter beads over the knots at the bottom.

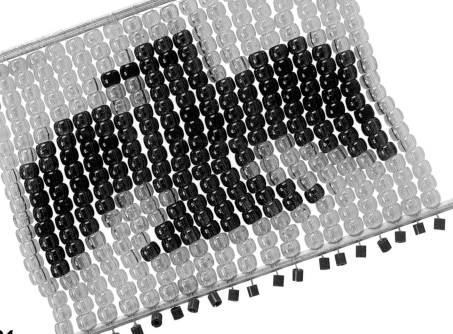

4 Tie a length of nylon thread to either end of the top skewer so you can hang up your sun catcher in the window or near a lamp.

Tube bracelets

These fabulous bracelets are made from plastic tubing stuffed with beads, tinsel and chocolate wrappers. You can buy tubing from the local hardware shop.

YOU WILL NEED

clear plastic
  tubing
assorted
  pink,
  orange,
  red and
  yellow tiny
  beads
pink plastic
  starter
  beads

small plug
  of dowel
  or bamboo
glue
scissors
wooden
  skewer or
  knitting
  needle

1 Point your fingers to make your hand thin, and then measure around the widest part of your hand. Cut a piece of tubing that length so you will be able to slip the finished bracelet on to your wrist.

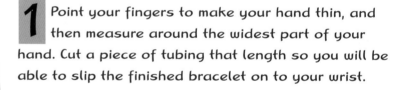

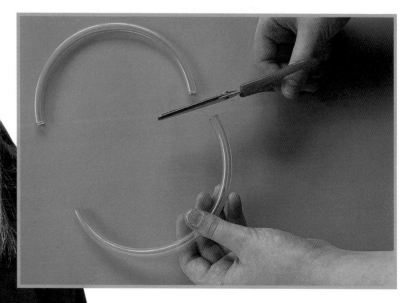

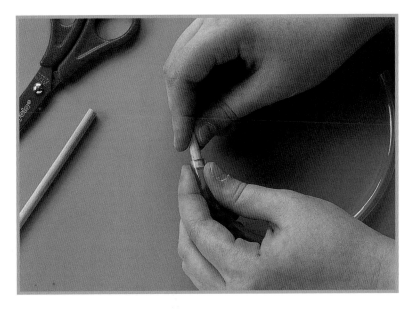

2 Ask an adult to cut a small bit of dowel or bamboo. Push it into one end of the plastic tube.

3 Use a skewer or a knitting needle to push beads into the tube. We have made a pattern by filling an inch of tube with tiny pink, orange and red beads, followed by a pink plastic starter bead. Repeat the pattern until the bracelet is nearly full. You can use tinsel and rolled-up foil from chocolates to make your bracelets sparkle if you like.

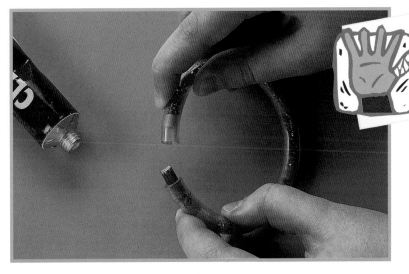

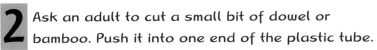

Ask an adult to help you cut the dowel.

4 Leave room at the end of the tube for the dowel plug. Dab glue around the plug, and push it into the free end of the tube. Make more bracelets so you can jangle them up and down your wrist.

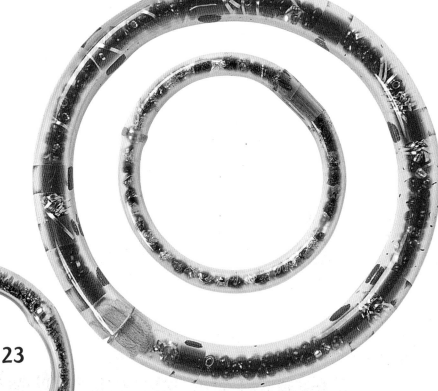

Bead wraps

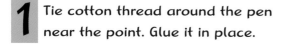

This bead craft brightens up all sorts of things. We have made a beaded pen and a drumstick. To make the drumstick, wrap a length of dowel with beads, then glue a big bead on to one end.

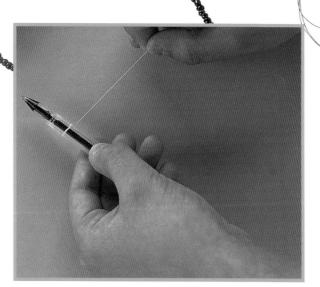

1 Tie cotton thread around the pen near the point. Glue it in place.

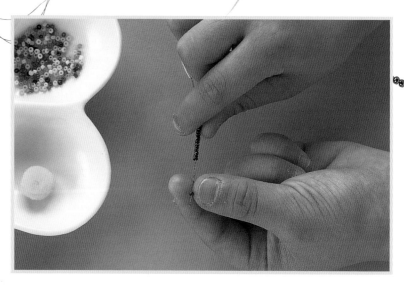

2 Begin to thread small beads on to the other end of the cotton thread.

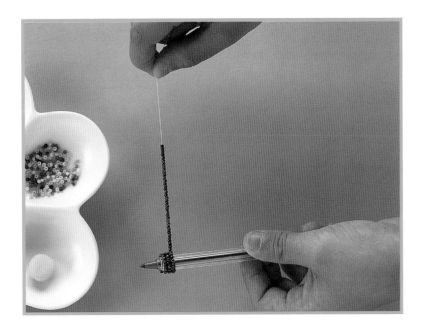

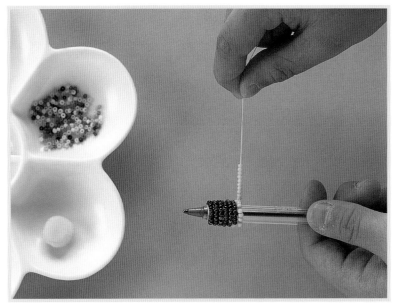

3 Dab glue on to the pen, and wind the beaded cotton thread tightly around the pen. You only need to glue on the first few rings of beads.

4 To make a pattern, count how many beads make a complete ring around the pen. It takes 16 beads to make a ring around our pen. We have made a yellow ring by threading on 16 yellow beads in a row.

5 Go on in the same way until you have nearly covered the pen. Dab glue on to the pen before you wrap the last few rings around. Wrap the remaining thread around the glued pen a few times, and then trim it. Glue a pompom on to the end for a fun finish.

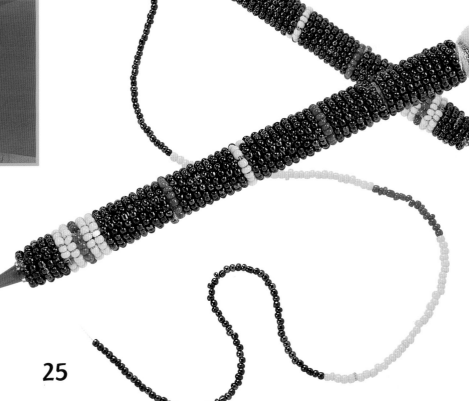

Beaded tiara

Choose beads that look like jewels to make a tiara. A tiara is a small half-crown that is usually made from diamonds set in silver or gold.

YOU WILL NEED

hair band with comb edge
three white pipe cleaners
five big pink beads

assorted smaller pink beads
glue
scissors

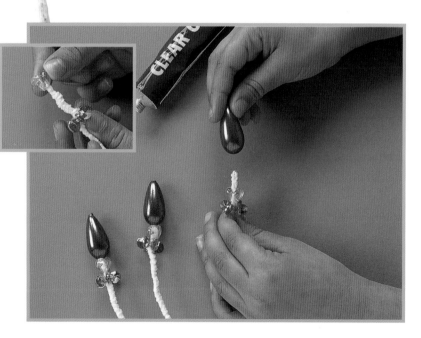

1 To make the centre prongs of the tiara, thread beads on to three pipe cleaners. We've used a flower-shaped bead, then a heart-shaped bead and then a big bead at the top, stuck on with glue.

2 Push one beaded pipe cleaner between the teeth of the comb in the centre of the hair band.

3 Wind the pipe cleaner around a few teeth to keep it in place. Push in the other two beaded pipe cleaners on either side.

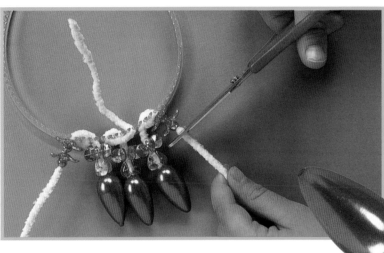

4 Point the two outer pipe cleaners up and thread on beads to make two more prongs for your tiara. Trim off the extra bits of pipe cleaner at the top.

5 To keep the prongs from falling out, wind the pipe-cleaner ends around each other at the base of the hairband and dab on glue to stick them in place.

Spider web

The design for this beaded web is based on a popular craft in Mexico and Bolivia called an Ojo de Dios (God's eye). It is made by winding wool around a cross shape.

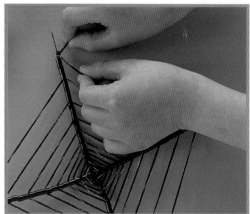

1 To make the web, tie two wires together in a cross using black wool. Wind the wool around each spike in turn. Once you have a solid centre, thread a black bead on to each spike, then wind the wool around each spike again.

2 Keep going until you have been around each wire four times. For the next two rounds thread on two beads as spacers. For the next two rounds use three beads, and for the last three rounds use four beads.

YOU WILL NEED

- black plastic starter beads
- black wool threaded with silver
- silver beads
- shiny silver stars
- two lengths of florist's wire
- glue
- button with four large holes
- black pipe cleaners
- thin tinsel
- big bead for the head
- assorted beads
- bottle cap
- toothpick

28

3 Tie the wool firmly to one spike to finish and then tie a loop so you can hang up the web. Glue on silver stars and silver beads to decorate.

4 To make the legs cut two black pipe cleaners in half. Bend one of these pieces in half and push the ends through the holes in a large button. Push the other three pieces through in the same way to make eight legs.

5 Cut the ends off a toothpick and glue a big bead on to one end to make a spider head. Place the toothpick under the button and wind two legs around it to keep it in place.

6 Dab glue on to a bottle cap and wind thin tinsel around it. Glue the cap to the top of the button to make the spider's body.

7 Glue on beads for the eyes and feet. Tie a length of wool to one of the spider's legs and tie the other end to the top spike of the web.

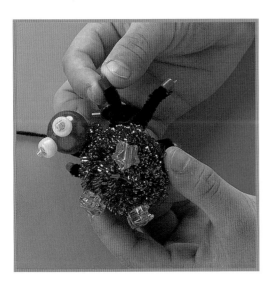

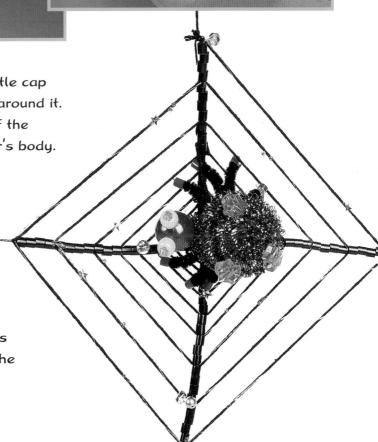

Patterns and diagrams

To make the Lampshade fringe, you will need to follow the diagram below. On the opposite page there is a diagram for you to follow to make the Sun catcher. The star patterns are for the Monster mancala game. Find out how to trace and make a pattern in the box on page 5.

**Lampshade fringe
page 16**

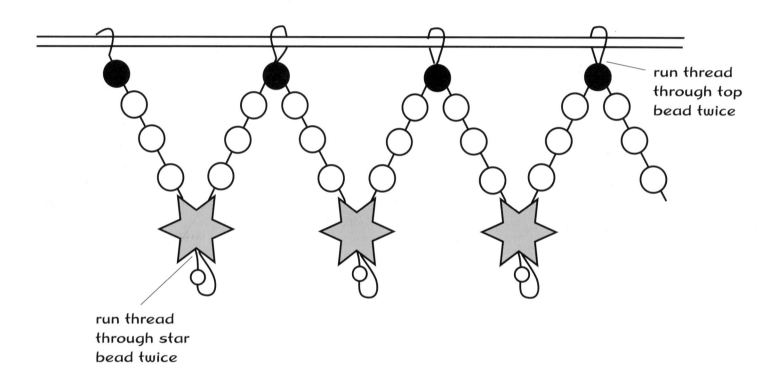

run thread
through top
bead twice

run thread
through star
bead twice

**big star to go in the
matchboxes**

**small star for the
hair spikes**

**Monster mancala
page 19**

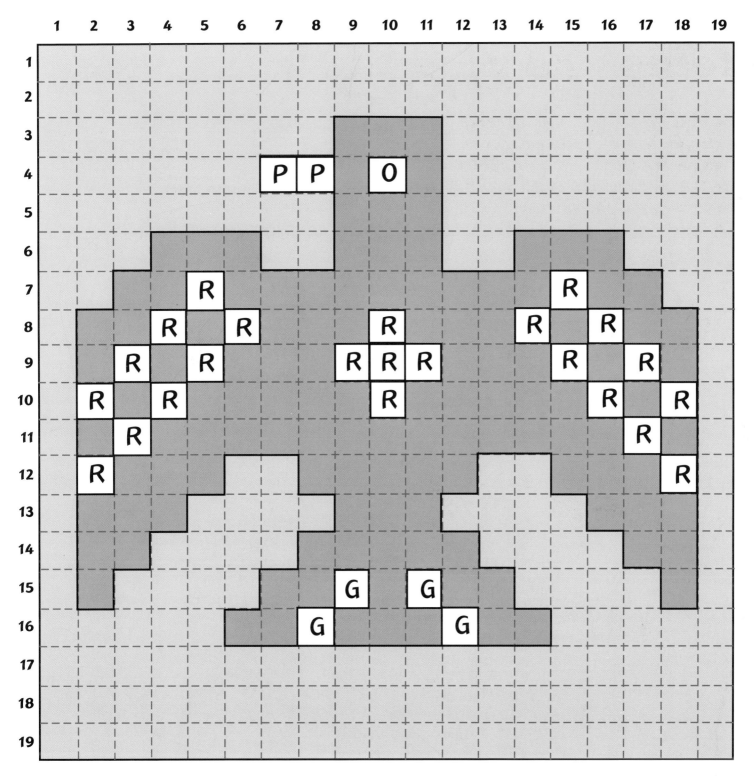

Sun catcher page 20

KEY

| P | = purple bead | | O | = orange bead | | R | = red bead | | G | = green bead |

= yellow bead   = blue bead

Index